COU... ...ORLD

 # KENYA

Ali Brownlie Bojang

W
FRANKLIN WATTS

This edition published in 2013 by
Franklin Watts
338 Euston Road
London NW1 3BH

Franklin Watts Australia
Level 17/207 Kent Street
Sydney NSW 2000

Produced for Franklin Watts by
White-Thomson Publishing Ltd
+44 (0) 845 362 8240
www.wtpub.co.uk

Series consultant: Rob Bowden
Editor: Sonya Newland
Designer: Amy Sparks
Picture researcher: Amy Sparks

A CIP catalogue record for this book is available
from the British Library.

Dewey Classification: 967.6'2043

ISBN 978 1 4451 1901 4
Library eBook ISBN 978 1 4451 1989 2

Printed in Malaysia

Franklin Watts is a division of Hachette
Children's Books, an Hachette UK company.

www.hachette.co.uk

Contents

Kenya is famous for its great natural beauty, which attracts visitors from all over the world, and it is one of Africa's main centres of banking and business. Although it suffers from poverty and civil unrest, Kenya is still one of Africa's most stable countries.

Where in the world?

Kenya lies on the Equator in East Africa. Although it is largely surrounded by land, it borders the Indian Ocean in the south-east. The ports along the coastline provide a gateway for trade and travel in this part of the African continent. In the west, where Kenya meets Uganda and Tanzania, lies Lake Victoria. Sudan and Ethiopia are situated to the north, and to the east is Somalia.

Historical global links

Throughout its long history, Kenya has had connections with other countries. Around the seventh century Arab traders set up towns along the Kenyan coast, and travellers came from as far away as China and Persia (now Iran). Although Arab influences declined in the nineteenth century, they are still evident today, particularly in Kenya's large Muslim population.

▶ *Kenya has land borders with Ethiopia to the north, Somalia to the east, Tanzania to the south, Uganda to the west and Sudan to the north-west.*

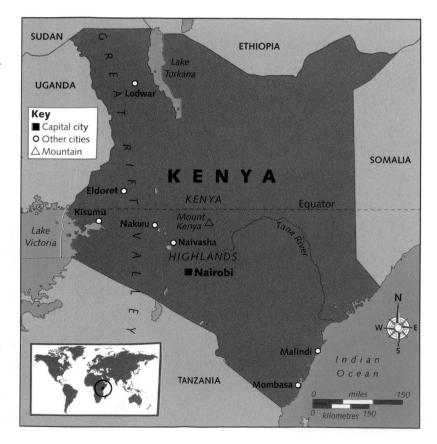

Key
■ Capital city
○ Other cities
△ Mountain

SUDAN
ETHIOPIA
UGANDA
Lodwar
Lake Turkana
SOMALIA
KENYA
Eldoret
KENYA
Equator
Kisumu
Nakuru
Mount Kenya △
Tana River
Lake Victoria
Naivasha
HIGHLANDS
■ **Nairobi**
GREAT RIFT VALLEY
Malindi
Indian Ocean
TANZANIA
Mombasa

miles 150
kilometres 150

The British in Kenya

The British began to arrive in Kenya in the eighteenth century, and by 1895 Britain ruled the country. Many British people came to live in Kenya, particularly in the west of the country in an area known as the Highlands. They established farms to grow tea and coffee. Thousands of local people, particularly the Maasai and Kikuyu tribes, were forced off their land by the new settlers. Using Kenyan and Asian workers, the British built railways to link the heart of the country to the coast and the ports, so that goods could be sent back to Britain. By 1920, there were 9,000 European settlers living in Kenya.

IT STARTED HERE

Human ancestors

In many parts of Kenya, scientists have found the remains of ape-like creatures believed to be very early ancestors of human beings. The earliest of these – fossils dating back more than 4.2 million years – have been discovered around the shores of Lake Turkana. Modern humans are believed to have originated here around 200,000 years ago.

▼ *Kenyans working on the building of a railway during the period of British rule.*

Independence

The British ruled Kenya for 67 years. Thousands of Kenyan soldiers fought for the British during World War I (1914–18), and they also fought in World War II (1939–45) in countries as far away as Burma. In the 1950s, some Kenyans – particularly members of the Kikuyu tribe – began to rebel against British rule. At first the British fought against the rebellion and imprisoned its leaders. Later, though, the British gave in to pressure and in 1963, Kenya became an independent country. Jomo Kenyatta, who had been involved in the Mau Mau rebellion, became the country's first president.

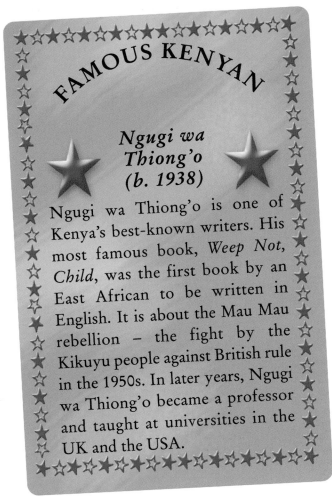

FAMOUS KENYAN

Ngugi wa Thiong'o (b. 1938)

Ngugi wa Thiong'o is one of Kenya's best-known writers. His most famous book, *Weep Not, Child*, was the first book by an East African to be written in English. It is about the Mau Mau rebellion – the fight by the Kikuyu people against British rule in the 1950s. In later years, Ngugi wa Thiong'o became a professor and taught at universities in the UK and the USA.

Kenya today

Kenya is famous for its stunning scenery and is one of the Africa's top tourist destinations. Its game parks, mountains and beautiful beaches are popular with visitors from all over the world. It has also gained some fame as the birthplace of the father of Barack Obama, the president of the USA.

◀ *Traditional dancers perform at a celebration in Nairobi commemorating Kenyan independence.*

▲ *The Bamburi cement depot at the port of Mombasa. Kenya's ports are vital for importing and exporting goods to and from East Africa.*

African leader

Today Kenya plays a leading role in areas such as trade and politics in Africa. Kenyan troops take part in peacekeeping missions in the neighbouring countries of Somalia and Sudan, where there are civil wars. Other neighbouring countries, such as landlocked Ethiopia and Uganda, rely on Kenya's ports and roads to send and receive goods from all over the world.

BASIC DATA
Official name: **Republic of Kenya**
Capital: **Nairobi**
Size: **582,650 sq km (224,962 sq miles)**
Population: **44,037,656**
Currency: **Kenyan shilling**

Landscapes and environment

Kenya can be split into three main regions, each with its own landscape and climate. These range from snow-capped mountains to sandy beaches, fertile farmland, barren deserts, open grasslands and lakes.

The north-east region

The north-east of Kenya is a very dry and hot region with sparse grassland known as savannah, thorn bushes and the occasional baobab tree. Very little grows here and not many people live in this area. Those that do are mainly nomadic pastoralists – people who keep cattle, goats or camels, and move from one feeding place to another to find the best land for grazing.

▼ *Herdsmen are the main inhabitants of Kenya's dry northern regions. This area suffers from droughts, so it is not ideal for farming or human settlement.*

The coast

Kenya's coastline stretches for 536 km (333 miles) along the south-east of the country. Here there are beautiful beaches lined with coral reefs. The climate is hot and humid all year. The beaches are popular with tourists, who also enjoy the fishing and water sports.

 Malindi is one of the largest coastal towns in Kenya, and attracts thousands of tourists every year, who go there to enjoy the warm weather and white-sand beaches.

The Highlands

The area known as the Highlands lies in the south-west of the country. This region is a large plateau of rolling grassland, ranging from 900–3,000 m (3,000–10,000 ft) high. Most of the farms in Kenya have been established here because the soil is fertile, there is high rainfall and the temperatures are cool at this altitude. Most of the population of Kenya lives in the Highlands, and it is home to the capital, Nairobi.

IT'S A FACT!

The Great Rift Valley is an enormous valley where the Earth's crust weakened and slowly tore itself apart 20 million years ago. The valley runs right through Kenya. In total, the valley stretches 6,000 km (3,700 miles) from as far north as Syria to Malawi in the south of Africa.

Rivers

Most of Kenya's rivers and small lakes dry up during the dry season. This leads to water shortages all over the country. The Tana River is the largest in the country, flowing 708 km (440 miles) into the Indian Ocean. The waters of Lake Victoria, the second largest freshwater lake in the world, feed into the White Nile in Uganda. Lake Victoria also has shores in Tanzania and Uganda, linking Kenya to these countries.

THE HOME OF...

Mount Kenya

Mount Kenya is the highest mountain in Kenya and the second highest in Africa, after Mount Kilimanjaro. It stands 5,199 m (17,057 ft) high and is actually an extinct volcano. The rivers that flow down Mount Kenya, including the Tana, are an important water source for the people of Kenya.

National parks and game parks

Kenya has two national parks that have been declared UNESCO World Heritage Sites – Lake Turkana National Park and Mount Kenya National Park. In total, Kenya has 65 national parks and reserves. Maasai Mara is one of the world's most famous national parks, and it is estimated that every year, between May and July, 1.3 million wildebeest and 400,000 zebra migrate here from Tanzania in search of water. Other animals found in Kenya include lions, antelopes, elephants, leopards, cheetahs, hyenas, rhinos, giraffes and buffaloes.

◀ *The 'Great Migration' sees wildebeest and zebra move between the Serengeti National Park in Tanzania and Maasai Mara in Kenya. Predators such as lions and hyenas follow the herds.*

▲ *Wangari Muta Maathai (centre), with members of the Green Belt Movement, which has planted 20 to 30 million trees in Africa.*

FAMOUS KENYAN

Wangari Muta Maathai (1940-2011)

In 2004, Wangari Muta Maathai became the first African woman to receive the Nobel Peace Prize for fighting to save the environment, and for peace and democracy. She became an elected member of the Kenyan parliament, and served as Assistant Minister for Environment and Natural Resources between 2003 and 2005.

Environmental issues

Kenya faces many environmental problems. Water pollution in the cities is caused by overcrowded shanty towns and factories, and in the countryside by the use of pesticides and fertilizers on the land. More than half of Kenya's forests have been cut down in the last 100 years, leading to soil erosion of the unprotected land. Efforts are now being made to address these issues by educating the people on the damage caused by pollution, and by encouraging more environmentally friendly farming and water management.

Population and migration

Kenya's population is made up of people who have always lived in the area and those who have travelled from other parts of Africa such as Sudan, Ethiopia and Somalia. There are also people who have come from Europe, the Middle East and Asia over hundreds of years.

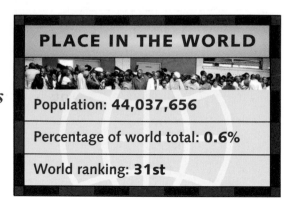

PLACE IN THE WORLD

Population: **44,037,656**

Percentage of world total: **0.6%**

World ranking: **31st**

Kenya's population

Although about 99 per cent of Kenyans are of African descent, there are small groups of Indians, Arabs and Europeans, particularly in the towns and cities. The number of people in Kenya has grown from about 6.5 million in 1950 to today's population of around 44 million. However, the rate at which the population is growing has dropped dramatically. Better healthcare means that parents are more confident that their children will survive, so they have smaller families. The drop in Kenya's birth rate is also due to the high number of people who die of the HIV/AIDS virus.

▼ *AIDS orphans from the Kibera slum in Nairobi are given food by community workers. The children are also educated about HIV/AIDS.*

IT'S A FACT!

Nearly half of the orphans in Kenya have been left without parents because of HIV/AIDS. In 2013, there were 1.1 million orphans in Kenya because one or both their parents had died from HIV/AIDS. That's the third highest number in the world.

Where do Kenyans live?

Seventy-five per cent of Kenyans live in the region between Nairobi and the Ugandan border. This covers only 10 per cent of the country's land area. Other groups live along the coast in the cities of Mombasa and Malindi. Most of the rest of the country is too dry or too rugged for many people to live there.

Nairobi

Around 3 million people live in Nairobi, Kenya's capital city. This is the most populated city in East Africa and the thirteenth largest on the continent. Nairobi is the main business centre in Kenya, and many international companies have their African headquarters there, including Coca-Cola, Citibank, Toyota and Google. One of the four international headquarters of the United Nations is also located in Nairobi.

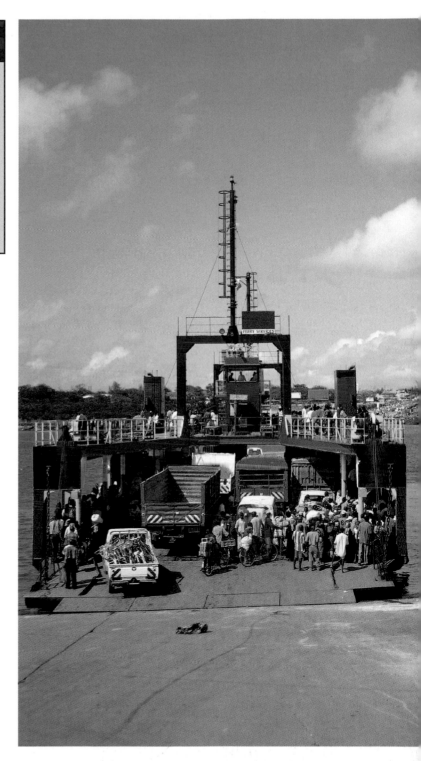

▲ *An early-morning ferry is crowded with locals on their way to work in Mombasa, Kenya's second largest city.*

Moving to the city

Nairobi is a vibrant and modern city. Cities attract young people from the countryside, who feel that they can earn more money there and find better career opportunities. About one-third of Kenya's population lives in urban areas. Unemployment in cities is very high, though, and more than half of Nairobi's population (around two million people) are forced to live in overcrowded shanty towns. The conditions they live in are sometimes worse than those in the villages they have left behind.

▼ *From the air, Nairobi looks like many modern cities, with skyscrapers and office blocks. On the outskirts, though, are slums housing thousands of people.*

GOING GLOBAL

There are about 100,000 Kenyan Asians, most of whom live in Nairobi and Mombasa. Asians have lived in East Africa for over 100 years, and they came in significant numbers during the period of British rule. Some came to work on the building of the railways. In 1968, about 70,000 of them fled to the UK after the Kenyan government refused to grant them work permits and licences for their businesses.

▲ *The Yara market in Kisumu, part of the Millennium Villages scheme, sells local produce and crafts, helping the villagers to support themselves.*

GLOBAL LEADER

Millennium Villages

Sauri, in western Kenya, is one of the first Millennium Villages. The Millennium Villages were started by the United Nations as part of the Millennium Development Goals to help poor villages work their way out of poverty with support from governments and foreign aid. Villages such as Sauri are models for villages all over the world to follow.

Leaving Kenya

Many Kenyans who can find jobs abroad leave for what they hope will be a better life. In 2011, the Office of National Statistics estimated that 133,000 people living in the UK were born in Kenya. This means that the UK has more Kenyan-born residents than French, Italian or Spanish. Many Kenyans who live abroad send money back to their families in Kenya, and this is an important source of income for Kenyans back home. In 2012, an estimated US$1.7 billion was sent to Kenya in the form of these 'remittances', contributing to Kenya's national income.

Refugees

Kenya has long been a refuge for people from neighbouring countries such as Sudan and Somalia. Almost half a million refugees live in three over-crowded camps in the dry north-eastern region of Kenya – one of the world's largest refugee settlements. In August 2012, the United Nations estimated that 630,000 refugees and asylum-seekers in total were living in Kenya.

Culture and lifestyles

There are 42 different ethnic groups in Kenya, each with its own language, music, dance and art. Most people see themselves as Kenyan, as well as a member of their ethnic group.

▼ The Samburu people are a semi-nomadic tribe from north-central Kenya. Here, Samburu men perform a traditional dance.

Ethnic groups

Kenya's largest ethnic group – at 22 per cent of the population – is the Kikuyu. Traditionally they were farmers, and many of them still are. However, in modern urban Kenya they also dominate business and politics. Other ethnic groups include the Luhya (14 per cent), Luo (13 per cent), Kalenjin (12 per cent), Kamba (11 per cent), Kisii (6 per cent) and Meru (6 per cent). Only one per cent of Kenya's population is non-African, made up of Asian, European or Arab people.

IT'S A FACT!

Swahili is a Bantu language (its proper name is KiSwahili), but about 35 per cent of it is made up of Arabic words. It also has words from German, Portuguese, Indian, English and French, due to contact in the past with all these different groups of people. It is Africa's most widely spoken African language, with 50 million speakers across East Africa and the Democratic Republic of the Congo.

Traditional and modern lifestyles

About two-thirds of Kenyans still live in the countryside. Although there have been many changes to life in rural areas over the centuries, some aspects of tribal lifestyles have remained the same. The pastoralists of the north, such as the Turkana, Pokot and Samburu peoples, measure their wealth by the number of cattle they own, and the Maasai are famous for their jewellery and cloth. However, life in cities is very different – similar to that in cities in many Western countries. Here there are shopping malls, supermarkets and fast-food restaurants. People work in modern offices, and pass time in Internet cafés and coffee shops.

▲ *In contrast to the traditional market places found in rural areas, city residents shop in modern, air-conditioned supermarkets.*

Music

Music is a good example of how the traditional mixes with the modern in Kenya. *Benga* is a form of music that combines jazz with local music, which usually features drums, rattles and shakers. International artists such as Sean Paul, Akon, Shaggy and Morgan Heritage have all performed in Kenya and have many fans there. Hip-hop and R&B music are very popular. Kenyan stars often mix Swahili and English with tribal languages in their songs.

Food

Kenyan food has been influenced by other countries. On the coast – an area with strong Arabian and Indian influences – people enjoy curries and spicy food. This kind of food is also popular in the towns and cities. In rural areas the staple food is *ugali*, a dish of mashed maize which, when the family can afford it, is eaten with a stew of beef or goat, although more usually with a vegetable stew. In the countryside and the shanty towns, people will gather round a large single bowl to eat. Wealthier Kenyans are just as likely to eat at expensive restaurants – or tuck into a takeaway hamburger or pizza.

◀ *Fruit and vegetables grow well in the Kenyan climate and are staples of Kenyan cooking.*

Religion

People in Kenya are free to follow whatever religion they choose. Over 80 per cent of Kenyans are Christian. Eleven per cent are Muslims and some of the remaining people are classified as having indigenous beliefs, based on their tribal group. Many people combine different beliefs in their religion. For example, a Christian or a Muslim may also hold indigenous African beliefs.

THE HOME OF...

The Safari Rally

Kenya's Safari Rally is considered to be the toughest cross-country car rally in the world. It is a two-day race through the Kenyan bush. Drivers have to contend with wild animals and pot-holed roads. Rally drivers from all over the world take part.

▲ *Kenyan runner David Rudisha (centre) ran an extraordinary 800 metres race at the 2012 London Olympics to take the gold medal.*

Sport

Kenyans love sport – especially football, which is the most popular one to watch and play. The British introduced the game of cricket in 1896 and this is quite popular, too. But Kenya is probably most famous for its record-breaking long-distance and middle-distance runners. Because they train at such high altitudes, Kenyan runners have an advantage over other athletes.

GOING GLOBAL

Many Kenyan athletes have changed their nationality following bids from rich countries in the Middle East such as Bahrain and Qatar. Their good international reputation means they are offered money and other benefits to represent these countries in competitions, and they often change their names to Arabic ones. Kenyan athletes are improving their adopted countries' sporting reputations.

Economy and trade

Kenya is one of the wealthiest countries in Africa. It is a vital centre of finance, transport and business for the whole of East Africa. Despite this, though, half of its population lives on less than US$1 a day. The discovery of oil in 2012 may provide an opportunity for Kenya to improve its economy.

IT'S A FACT!

Kenya has particularly close ties with its neighbours Tanzania and Uganda. Together these countries established the East African Community, an organization set up to help these countries cooperate and trade with each other. In 2007, Burundi and Rwanda joined the Community as full members.

The farming industry

Farming is still the most important part of the Kenyan economy – 75 per cent of the workforce is involved in farming, but only 12 per cent of these are involved in growing cash crops (crops grown especially for export). The rest are small farmers, who grow just enough of crops like beans, cassava, potatoes, maize and sorghum to feed their families.

▼ *Tea-pickers work on a plantation in Limuru, central Kenya. Tea and coffee plantations were established here during the period of British rule.*

Cash crops

Cash crops are responsible for more than 50 per cent of Kenya's export earnings. Growing vegetables, herbs, spices and flowers for export is big business. Kenya is Africa's leading producer of tea, and fourth in the world behind India, China and Sri Lanka. Coffee is also an important export, and is found in supermarkets and coffee shops all over the USA and Europe. Other farming exports include tobacco, sugar and cotton. Sugar and cotton production have suffered in recent years, as world prices have dropped and other countries have been able to produce cheaper cotton (China) and sugar (Brazil).

GOING GLOBAL

One of Kenya's growing export industries is cut flowers, such as roses and carnations. The flower-growing industry employs at least 500,000 Kenyans. However, growing flowers uses up precious water supplies and takes up land that could be used for growing food crops. To make sure the flowers arrive fresh they are transported by air, which has a negative impact on the environment. Some people argue that flowers flown from Africa use less energy overall than those produced in Europe because they are not grown in heated greenhouses.

▲ *A worker at a flower farm in Naivasha pushes a cart of red roses, ready to be exported to Europe in time for Valentine's Day.*

Tourism

Tourism brings the most foreign income into Kenya. In 2011, well over a million tourists visited Kenya. Visitors from the UK formed the largest national group, followed by those from the USA and Italy. Increasing numbers of visitors, however, are travelling from countries such as China, South Korea and India. Tourism is a growing industry, but it is not developing as quickly as it might. People are often afraid to travel to Kenya because there have been terrorist attacks and riots there. There are other countries in Africa, especially South Africa, that have attractions similar to those in Kenya, so tourists may choose to go there instead if the situation in Kenya is not made more stable.

▲ *The main tourist attractions in Kenya are wildlife safaris, where people are taken on tours across the savannah to see animals such as lions and elephants.*

IT'S A FACT!

China has taken a keen interest in oil exploration in Africa, and the Kenyan government has given the China National Offshore Oil Company exclusive rights to look for oil in the Mandera area of north-east Kenya. China now controls 28 per cent of the total area in Kenya set aside for oil exploration.

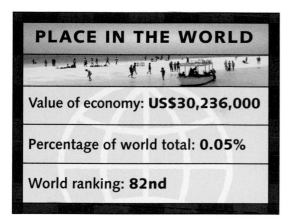

PLACE IN THE WORLD

Value of economy:	**US$30,236,000**
Percentage of world total:	**0.05%**
World ranking:	**82nd**

▼ *The debt built up by the Kenyan government puts a strain on the economy and means that many Kenyan children grow up in poverty.*

Corruption

Kenya is wealthier than most African countries, and it has the potential to be an economically successful country. However, it has suffered some setbacks. This has mainly been caused by the corruption of government officials, who took money for awarding government contracts. This corruption gave Kenya a bad reputation around the world. Although efforts have been made to stop corruption, the reforms have not been very successful, and the problem is still widespread.

Debt

Under the former president, Daniel arap Moi, Kenya built up huge debts that now stand at nearly US$7 billion. This means that Kenya must pay back huge amounts of money to wealthier countries in debt repayments every year, which puts a great strain on the country's economy.

Kenya is a republic, which means that it is not ruled by a king or queen, but by a government elected by the people. The president is the head of the government. Elections are held at least every five years to choose a president and members of parliament.

'All pull together'

When Jomo Kenyatta became president in 1963, he wanted to build a new Kenya. He hoped to create a united country based on the Swahili word *Harambee*, which means 'all pull together'. To begin with he allowed other political parties to exist in Kenya – just like in countries such as the UK and USA – but by 1969 Kenyatta had banned all other parties. His political party was the only one allowed, and he had all the power. Even after Kenyatta died in 1978, his successor, Daniel arap Moi, continued to rule in the same way. Western countries began to pressurise the Kenyan government to make politics more fair, and in 1991 other political parties were allowed.

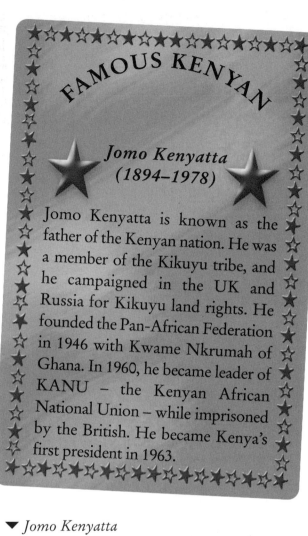

FAMOUS KENYAN

Jomo Kenyatta (1894–1978)

Jomo Kenyatta is known as the father of the Kenyan nation. He was a member of the Kikuyu tribe, and he campaigned in the UK and Russia for Kikuyu land rights. He founded the Pan-African Federation in 1946 with Kwame Nkrumah of Ghana. In 1960, he became leader of KANU – the Kenyan African National Union – while imprisoned by the British. He became Kenya's first president in 1963.

▼ *Jomo Kenyatta was the first president of an independent Kenya.*

Constitution and parliament

In 2010 a new constitution was adopted in Kenya. This brought in some limits to the power of the president and devolved power and resources to forty-seven newly created counties. The Kenyan parliament is known as the National Assembly (or Bunge) and it has recently been expanded to 350 members, including 290 elected ones, 47 elected women, 12 members nominated by the president and the Speaker.

▲ *Nairobi's City Hall is the centre of local government for the province of Nairobi. Local governments make decisions about issues such as healthcare and education.*

In addition, there is the senate, consisting of 67 elected members and the Speaker.

IT'S A FACT!

Kenya is a member of several international groups, including the United Nations, the Commonwealth, the African Union, the World Trade Organization and the East African Community. Membership of organizations like these means that Kenya has a say about important issues that affect countries worldwide.

Disputed elections

Elections in 2007 and 2008 were followed by riots and violence. The United Nations, including former UN Secretary General Kofi Annan, helped to resolve the issues and it was decided that the different political parties should share power in a coalition government. This cross-party government worked together to draw up the new constitution, adopted in 2010. The 2013 elections passed off without violence and resulted in victory for Uhuru Kenyatta, the son of Jomo Kenyatta (see page 24).

▶ *Although everyone over the age of 18 can vote in Kenya, they often have to queue for hours to do so, a problem that the United Nations would like the Kenyan government to address.*

GOING GLOBAL

Kenya has played an important role in bringing peace to – and keeping peace in – other countries, especially war-torn African countries. Kenya is one of the 12 countries that account for 75 per cent of the total UN forces. In 2005 it helped bring about an end to a civil war in Sudan, and it has helped prevent fighting in Somalia from spreading across the border. Kenyan troops and police have also served in Liberia and Sierra Leone.

Human rights

Since Mwai Kibaki came to power in 2002, the government has worked to improve human rights in Kenya. When Daniel arap Moi was president, Kenya did not have a good reputation in this area. People who criticized the government were often arrested, held without trial and tortured. In 2003, the Kenya National Human Rights Commission was set up to ensure that international human rights standards were met. In 2010, a new constitution was implemented, alongside police and justice reforms. A UN team complimented the Kenyan government on the running of its 2013 election, which largely passed without the violence that scarred the previous elections.

▼ *A Kenyan peacekeeping soldier on a mission in Eritrea, in north-east Africa. UN peacekeeping forces can be recognized by their blue helmets.*

Kenya has the potential to be a stable and successful country. To achieve this, it must continue to work closely with other countries to help build its economy. With a strong economy, all Kenyans may benefit and be able to improve their standards of living.

IT'S A FACT!

Vision 2030 is a plan for Kenya's economy over the next 20 years in which money will be spent developing areas such as tourism, farming and information technology. Part of Vision 2030 is a bid for Kenya to host the Olympic Games in 2028.

Ethnic conflicts

Differences and conflict between the ethnic groups are threatening Kenya's political stability. If there is more unrest, the tourist industry could suffer further, as people will be afraid to visit Kenya. Global events that Kenya may have no control over, such as terrorist incidents or global diseases that stop people travelling, could also affect the tourist industry.

▼ *Tourists come to see tribes like the Maasai living their traditional lifestyles. But what will happen if tourists are put off by political instability?*

▲ *Kenyans celebrate the election of Barack Obama as US president. Many believe that Kenya will benefit in some way from this.*

The new constitution

Many people in Kenya hope that the new constitution, adopted in 2010, will stop corruption in the higher levels of government as well as conflict between different tribal groups. Alongside the new constitution, significant reforms are being implemented to improve the judicial system as well as the police force, and to provide more checks and balances on presidential power.

International co-operation

Kenya's economic future could also lie in the development of the East African Community. Kenya is a key member of this organization, which encourages members to work together in the areas of politics and economics. This will create more trade and could lead to a common system of money and political unity. With more than 50 per cent of Kenyans living on less than US$1 a day, however, battling poverty must be a priority for the future.

Glossary

cash crops crops that are grown especially to be exported to other countries.

Christianity a religion that follows the teachings of Jesus Christ.

civil war when groups of people within a country fight one another.

continent one of the Earth's seven great land masses – Africa, Asia, Australia, Europe, North America, South America and Antarctica.

coral reefs underwater structures formed from the remains and skeletons of sea creatures.

economy the financial system of a country or region, including how much money is made from the production and sale of goods and services.

Equator an imaginary circle around the Earth that divides it into northern and southern hemispheres.

ethnic group a group of people who identify with each other and feel they share a history.

export to transport products or materials abroad for sale or trade.

GDP gross domestic product – the total value of all goods and services produced in a country in a given year.

Islam a religion with belief in one god (Allah) and his last prophet, Muhammad.

Mau Mau a secret society of Kikuyus that led a rebellion against the ruling Europeans in Kenya in the 1950s.

migrate to move from one place to another.

Muslim someone who follows the religion of Islam.

nomadic moving from place to place.

pastoralist someone who keeps livestock.

plateau a raised area of land, usually fairly flat and sometimes also called 'tableland'.

pollution spoiling the environment with man-made waste such as vehicle emissions, waste gases from factories, or chemicals from fertilizers.

rebellion an organized resistance to a government.

refugee someone who flees from war, oppression or persecution in search of refuge and safety.

republic a form of government in which a country is ruled not by a king or queen but by officials elected by the people.

rural relating to the countryside.

safari a Swahili word meaning a trip – usually referring to an overland journey to look for wildlife.

urban something that is related to or located in a city.

Further information

Books

Kenya (Country Files)
by Michael Graham
(Franklin Watts, 2006)

Kenya (Country Insights)
by Mairead Dunne, Wambui Kariri and
Eric Nyanjom
(Wayland, 2008)

Kenya (Destination Detectives)
by Rob Bowden
(Raintree Publishers, 2006)

Kenya (Discover Countries)
by Chris Ward
(Wayland, 2010)

Living in Kenya
by Ruth Thomson
(Franklin Watts, 2005)

We're from Kenya (Young Explorer)
by Vicky Parker
(Heinemann, 2006)

Websites

http://www.oxfam.org.uk/coolplanet/kidsweb/
world/kenya/index.htm
Oxfam's 'Cool Planet' page on Kenya, with all sorts
of information about the history, geography and
people of the country.

http://www.globaleye.org.uk/primary_spring01/
focuson/kenya.html
The effects of tourism on Kenya.

http://www.tourism.go.ke
The official website of Kenya's Ministry of Tourism.

http://www.socialstudiesforkids.com/subjects/
economics.htm
Get to grips with economics on this site where topics
such as money, trade and budgets are explained.

*Every effort has been made by the publisher to ensure
that these websites contain no inappropriate or offensive
material. However, because of the nature of the Internet,
it is impossible to guarantee that the content of these sites
will not be altered. We strongly advise that Internet access
is supervised by a responsible adult.*

Index

Numbers in **bold** indicate pictures